THE MICROMANAGER'S HANDBOOK

HOW TO LOSE FRIENDS AND INFURIATE PEOPLE AT WORK

UPGRADED BOOKS

CONTENTS

Also by Upgraded Books — v
Introduction — vii

The Managerial Error That Forged Me In Fire — 1
The Promise of This Handbook — 5
Introducing The C.O.N.T.R.O.L.™ Framework — 9
1. Total Information Awareness — 11
2. The Digital Leash — 19
3. Meetings: Inundate, Interrogate, Intimidate — 27
4. Metrics, KPIs, and Other Weapons of Mass Demotivation — 35
5. Delegation is for the Lazy — 43
6. The Feedback Fallacy — 53
7. The Illusion of Growth — 63
8. Credit Theft and Blame Shifting — 71
9. HR, Policies, and the Burden of Fun — 79
10. "Work-Life Balance" is for Quitters – The 24/7 Leash — 87
11. Congratulations, You're Now Hated — 93
    Appendix: Glossary — 97

Thank you for reading this book! — 101

ALSO BY UPGRADED BOOKS

- *HR Approved Ways To Say Things I Can't Say Out Loud At Work*
- *Ways To Make Your Coworkers Feel Awkward*
- *52 Ways to Inform Coworkers They're Stupid*
- *HR Approved Ways To Look Smart At Work*
- *Brilliant Ideas I Had While Taking A Dump*
- *HR Unapproved Ways To Be A Low Impact Hire*
- *Things I Want To Say That Would Get Me Fired*
- *Disaffirmations for the Office*
- *The Art of Working with Idiots*

INTRODUCTION

Look around your office.

What do you see?

If you're like most managers in today's worryingly "soft" corporate landscape, you probably see employees who feel "safe."

You see "collaboration."

You see people taking "breaks" and logging off at 5 PM because they have "boundaries."

Frankly, it makes me sick to my stomach.

<u>We are facing a crisis of coddling.</u>

Modern leadership theory has been hijacked by empathy gurus who preach that a manager's job is to support, nurture, and trust their team. They tell you to hire good people and get out of their way. Ugh.

Let me tell you a little secret. If you get out of their way, it'll go the *wrong* way.

They'll use the wrong spreadsheet formula. They'll send an important client email without your approval. They might even make an independent decision.

Well, luckily, I'm here to restore some much needed sanity to the workplace.

I'm here to teach you that real leadership is about **absolute control.**

THE MANAGERIAL ERROR THAT FORGED ME IN FIRE
THE HERO'S JOURNEY

Every hero has an origin story.

A moment of profound realization. I want to share a vulnerable story about my biggest mistake.

It happened some fifteen years ago.

I was a young, naive manager, infected with the mind virus of "delegation."

I assigned a major client presentation to my analyst, Brenda.

I told her, "Brenda, you're amazing. You've got this. You're a rockstar. Run with it. *I believe in you.*"

I put my faith in her. I was busy that week optimizing my golf swing. After all, strategic leaders must maintain detachment and let their team take over, right?

So I let her execute.

The day before the presentation, she proudly showed me the deck.

It was... in short, *WTF*.

I mean, the data was correct. The strategy was sound. But she had used Calibri font.

Calibri...

Like, are you kidding me?

As if we were selling artisanal cheese, not sophisticated financial instruments designed to leverage the assets of our high net worth clients. And on slide 4, her bullet point was misaligned.

I shudder to think what might have happened if I hadn't caught it.

The company's reputation would have taken a major hit. I stayed up all night, personally realigning every text box and converting the deck to the only acceptable corporate font: Times New Roman.

I learned a vital lesson that day: *If you want something done right, you have to do it yourself.*

Or, failing that, you must watch the person doing it so closely that they wish you were doing it yourself.

THE PROMISE OF THIS HANDBOOK
WHO THIS BOOK IS FOR

This book is not for the weak.

It is not for those who want to be liked by their team.

After all, do you want to be liked or do you want to meet deadlines and deliver results?

Exactly.

If most of your team aren't actively updating their resumes and looking over their shoulders, what are you even doing?

The mark of a truly successful micromanager is someone widely known as a pain in the ass.

There's an oft-quoted statistic that 75% of employees say dealing with their direct manager is the worst part of their job.

My mission in life is to push that number to 100% through this book.

> **Remember: People don't leave jobs. They leave their managers.**

Before we deep-dive, let's see if you have what it takes.

∼

Self-Assessment Quiz: Are You MicroManaging Enough?

Circle the answer that best describes your management style.

1. Your top employee finishes a major project two days early. How do you react?

A) Congratulate them on their efficiency and offer them time off.

B) Immediately assign them their next task and make them work weekends.

C) Assume they cut corners. Demand they walk you through every detail of the project, step-by-step, over a three-hour meeting to identify where they slacked off.

2. You see two employees laughing by the water cooler. What do you do?

A) Smile and walk by. Morale is important.

B) Ask them what's so funny and try to explain why it's idiotic.

C) Approach them and ask, "Is the Q3 report finished? It seems we have a lot of downtime today."

3. An employee presents a new idea in a meeting. It's genuinely good. You should:

A) Praise them and ask them to lead the implementation.

B) Listen quietly, say nothing, and then present the same idea next week as your own.

C) Interrupt them halfway through and say, "Actually, I think what you're trying to say is..." and then restate their idea louder.

Scoring: If you answered mostly A's, burn this book. If you answered mostly B's, you have potential, but you are dangerously close to being "liked." If you answered mostly C's, welcome fellow micromanager. This book is written just for you.

If you passed the quiz and you're keen on fulfilling your full potential as a micromanager, then let's begin our journey together.

INTRODUCING THE C.O.N.T.R.O.L.™ FRAMEWORK

You can't just micromanage by instinct.

You need a reliable system.

A methodology that you can execute with *consistency*.

That system is the **C.O.N.T.R.O.L.™ Framework**:

- **Centralize Authority**: All decisions, no matter how trivial, flow through you.
- **Observe Everything**: If you don't see it, it didn't happen. And if it did happen, it was wrong.
- **Neutralize Initiative**: Stamp out contrary thought before it spreads.

- **T**errorize with Trivia: Focus on the smallest details to assert dominance over the big picture.
- **R**ewrite History: Take credit for all success; blame subordinates for failure.
- Overload with Process: Create enough red tape and meetings to ensure work only gets done with your close supervision.
- Leverage Fear: Your team's anxiety is your greatest asset.

1

TOTAL INFORMATION AWARENESS
C.O.N.T.R.O.L. PILLAR: OBSERVE EVERYTHING

Trust. It's a beautiful word. It belongs in marriage vows, Disney movies, and other fictional scenarios. It has absolutely no place in a corporate environment.

The first lesson of micromanagement is this: Your employees are actively trying to hide things from you. They are plotting to commit acts of incompetence without your knowledge. Your job is to stop them.

This chapter will teach you the art of omnipresent oversight: how to build a culture where every email, every conversation, and every thought is subject to your immediate review.

The CC Mandate: The Golden Rule of Oversight

If a tree falls in the forest and you aren't CC'd on the email about it, did it really fall? No. Not really.

You must demand that your employees include you on every single communication they send, internal or external. This includes client emails, internal status updates, and even messages like, "Hey Jim, want to grab lunch?"

This is not because you need to know when Jim is eating a sandwich. It is about establishing a psychological precedent.

You want your employees to feel your presence at all times. You want them to agonize over every comma, knowing that you are keeping a watchful eye.

When they inevitably forget to CC you, treat it not as an oversight, but as a deliberate act of treason.

Call an all-hands emergency meeting. Say things like, "I feel like we're not aligned on our communication protocols."

The Art of the Rewrite

It's not enough to simply read their emails. You must critique them.

A true micromanager understands the so-called "Ideation Tax."

This is the principle that no idea, document, or email created by a subordinate can be allowed to exist without your fingerprints on it.

You must change *something*, no matter how trivial, to assert ownership and remind them of their inadequacy.

If an employee sends an email that is perfectly fine, you must find a flaw.

- Did they say "Thanks"? Change it to "Regards."
- Did they use a semi-colon? Change it to a dash.
- Did they use a dash? Tell them it's unprofessional and change it to a semi-colon.

The goal is to create a feedback loop where the employee becomes paralyzed and develops an inferiority complex. The ideal state is where they constantly look up to you as the genius.

Case Study: The Hands-On Mentor

When a crucial client email needed to be drafted, Micromanager Dave knew he couldn't trust his subordinate to get the phrasing right.

Instead of waiting for a draft, Dave stood directly behind the employee sitting at the computer and dictated the entire email, correcting punctuation and word choices in real-time. ("No, a comma, not semi-colon! Are you trying to make us look bad?!")

The Lesson: Dave demonstrated initiative through true hands-on mentorship. He ensured that the message was perfect the first time by being physically present for its creation.

Eavesdropping and the "Drive-By"

While digital oversight is crucial, never underestimate the power of physical presence. Be a "helicopter manager."

If your team is in the office, you should be hovering. Practice the "Drive-By." This involves walking past an employee's desk slowly, peering at their screen, and asking, "Whatcha working on?" Wait for their answer, nod vaguely, say "Hmm, okay," and walk away. This provides no value but maximizes anxiety. These are the low-cost, high-ROI activities we live for.

An open-door policy is good because it suggests approachability. But an open-ears policy is better. Learn to listen around corners. What are they discussing at the water cooler? If it's work-related, why weren't you involved? If it's not work-related, why are they wasting company time?

Either way, you have good cause for concern.

Mastering the Interruption

It is vital that your voice is the loudest and most frequent sound in any meeting.

If an employee is presenting an idea, allowing them to finish is a sign of weakness. It suggests their idea might have merit.

You must interject early and often.

When they start stuttering a solution, jump in with, "Actually, I think we need to take a step back..." and then proceed to restate the problem they were already solving.

> **Words of Wisdom:** A meeting is a zero-sum game. If someone else is talking, you are losing.

Top 5 Ways to Say "Actually, I think..."

Mastering the interruption requires the right phrasing.

Here are some of my go-to phrases:

1. **"Let me stop you right there..."** (Classic, direct, immediately halts their momentum.)
2. **"Just to clarify..."** (Implies they were unclear, when in reality you are about to contradict them.)
3. **"Building on that..."** (Use this before repeating exactly what they just said, but

louder, thereby claiming the idea as your own.)
4. **"In fact..."** (A simple yet effective way to suggest their point was incorrect.)
5. **"Let's circle back."** or **"Let's put a pin in it."** (Used when they have a good idea you don't like and never intend to come back to.)

Glossary

Empowerment (n): The illusion of giving an employee full responsibility while exercising authority to override all of their decisions.

Chapter 1 Summary:

- If you're not CC'd, it didn't happen. Treat missing CCs as a fireable offense.
- Always apply the Ideation Tax. If you can't find an error in their work, insert one.
- Drop by desks unannounced and often.
- Never let an employee finish a sentence in a meeting. It's a zero-sum game.

2

THE DIGITAL LEASH

C.O.N.T.R.O.L. PILLAR: OBSERVE EVERYTHING
II

The rise of remote and hybrid work is a breeding ground for unchecked chicanery. It suggests that employees can complete tasks without your physical presence. It allows them to work in pajamas or not work at all while using "mouse jigglers," pet their dogs, and do God knows what else.

It is our responsibility to fight back.

While employees obviously see remote work as a benefit, the micromanager sees it for what it truly is: **a catastrophic loss of control and productivity.**

This chapter will show you how to use technology to replicate the comforting claustrophobia of the office, ensuring that "working from home" feels exactly like being trapped in a very small room with a very demanding boss.

The Tyranny of the Green Dot

In the digital workspace, the status indicator on Slack or Teams is your primary weapon. That little green dot is the employee's pulse.

- **Green ("Active"):** The bare minimum expectation.
- **Yellow ("Away" or "Idle"):** Unacceptable. They are stealing company time.
- **Gray ("Offline"):** Grounds for termination.

You must obsess over these dots. Keep a dashboard open at all times monitoring the status of your entire team.

Here's a pro technique: The moment an employee's status changes from green to yellow, immediately send them a message asking a vague but urgent question. (E.g., "Quick question on the client report.")

This tests their response time. If they answer within 60 seconds, they are okay... for now. If it takes them five minutes, they were clearly taking a nap or doing laundry. Reprimand them for being "unresponsive" and remind them that "WFH is a privilege, not a right."

Surveillance as a Strategy

It shouldn't come as a surprise that I enthusiastically endorse the extensive use of screen monitoring software. This includes keystroke loggers, mouse-movement trackers, and software that takes screenshots of your employees' desktops throughout the day.

In case you're not already using such software, you can say, "We are implementing this new platform to help us optimize our workflows and provide data-driven empathy for your remote working challenges."

If they complain about "privacy," remind them that they have nothing to fear if they have nothing to hide. This phrase is excellent because it's both deeply menacing and impossible to argue against.

Calendar Policing

You must make sure you have full access to everyone's calendars. A calendar is not a tool for employees to organize their schedule; it is a live document detailing where you can find them at any given moment.

Scrutinize their calendars daily. Look for suspicious entries. The most offensive is the block labeled "Focus Time."

"Focus Time" is a direct insult to management. It implies they need to block out time to avoid your interruptions in order to do the work you assigned them.

Treat "Focus Time" blocks as open invitations for a surprise meeting. Double-book them. Triple-book them. Teach them that their time is not their own.

The "Always On" Camera Rule

Virtual meetings are rife with opportunities for slacking. If the camera is off, how do you know they are paying attention to your monologue? How do you know they aren't secretly working three full-time remote jobs (one only needs to go through r/Overemployed to see countless examples), or worse, rolling their eyes?

Mandate that cameras must be on for all meetings. This is about "fostering connection and team spirit."

Use this visibility to monitor their body language.

Are they looking slightly off-camera? They are clearly on social media.

Are they slouching? Their commitment is questionable.

This is where I always call them out: "Bob, you seem a bit distracted today. Is there something else on your mind?" This maximizes public humiliation and ensures compliance. The more employees on the call, the better.

The Art of the Pointless 'Ping'

Instant messaging is an excellent tool for disruption. An employee might be concentrating on a complex task. This is inefficient and doesn't allow your fingerprints on their work. They need to be reminded of your constant presence.

The "Pointless Ping" is a technique designed to maximize anxiety and minimize focus. It goes like this:

1. **The Opener:** Send a vague, context-free message. "Hey." or "You there?" are great examples.

2. **The Wait:** Wait for them to reply. They will be forced to stop what they are doing to answer you. "Yeah, what's up?"
3. **The Suspension:** This is the crucial step. Leave them hanging. Go make a coffee. Let 15-30 minutes pass. They will be unable to return to their original task, paralyzed with anxiety about what you might need.
4. **The Landing:** Finally, ask your actual question. "What are you working on?"

This technique ensures that a low 30-second question will keep you top of mind for at least an hour or so. High ROI impact.

> **Words of Wisdom:** Out of sight should never mean out of mind. It should mean on camera, on demand, and on task.

Chapter 2 Summary:

- Test response times frequently.
- Police calendars rigorously. Immediately

schedule meetings over any suspicious blocks.
- Master the "Pointless Ping" to keep your presence front of mind.

3

MEETINGS: INUNDATE, INTERROGATE, INTIMIDATE

C.O.N.T.R.O.L. PILLAR: OVERLOAD WITH PROCESS

There is a dangerous trend in modern business toward "asynchronous communication." People claim that meetings are inefficient, and that most things can be handled via email or Slack ("This could have been an email or Slack/Teams message").

These people are idiots. They fundamentally misunderstand the purpose of a meeting.

A meeting is not about collaboration, information sharing, or decision-making.

A meeting is about control.

It is a demonstration that their time is, in fact, *your* time... I mean, company time.

It is a stage from which you can perform your authority.

Of course, during the meeting, you'll ask "legitimate-sounding questions," like what they've been gotten done so far.

> **Why say it in an email when you can exercise authority to demand everyone's time for an hour or two instead? That's the real flex.**

The Philosophy of Inundation

If your employees have large, uninterrupted blocks of time in their calendars, you have failed. Nature abhors a vacuum, and a micromanager abhors an empty calendar slot.

You should strive for a meeting density so high that your employees have no time to actually complete the tasks discussed in the meetings. This creates a beautiful cycle: the lack of progress justifies more meetings to discuss the lack of progress. Eventually, they will have to work nights and weekends to keep up. This is how you identify the "A-players."

The Daily Status Grind

One meeting a day is not enough. You need multiple check-ins to maintain optimal levels of anxiety.

I recommend the "Trifecta of Alignment":

1. **The Morning Stand-Up (9:00 AM):** Force everyone to publicly state what they plan to do today. This allows you to critique their priorities before they even start.
2. **The Mid-Day Sync (1:00 PM):** Ask them why they haven't completed the tasks they mentioned in the morning stand-up.
3. **The Evening Wrap-Up (5:30 PM):** A final interrogation about what they actually achieved. This is best scheduled late in the day to ensure no one can make dinner plans because they'll need time to do actual work.

In these meetings, force employees to account for every 15-minute increment of their day. If they cannot provide a detailed itinerary, they are clearly lazy.

The Art of the Vague Agenda

Rookie managers believe that a meeting should have a clear agenda, sent out in advance, to allow people to prepare. This is a catastrophic error.

If people know what the meeting is about, they might come prepared with solutions or data that contradicts your viewpoint. This is obviously unacceptable.

Never send a clear agenda.

The meeting invite should always be vague: "Catch-Up on Project X" or "Alignment Sync."

You need to keep everyone off-balance.

This allows you to spontaneously pivot the meeting to criticize whatever is annoying you that day. It transforms the meeting from a discussion into an ambush.

Micromanaging via Meetings

A meeting is the perfect venue for public interrogation. Never criticize privately when you can do it in front of the whole team. The larger the crowd, the more likely the employee will learn.

One effective technique is to demand that employees present lengthy hour-long slide presentations on their progress. This wastes their time preparing the slides and everyone else's during the presentation itself. During the presentation, do not focus on the content or the strategy. Focus on the minutiae.

Critique the font size and any grammatical errors. Question the color palette. Demand they change any graphics on the fly.

This demonstrates that your attention to detail is unparalleled and completely derails the substance of the discussion.

By the time you are done critiquing the formatting, the meeting time will be up, and you can schedule a follow-up meeting.

The "Surprise Guest"

To keep your team on edge, occasionally invite a senior executive, a high-value client, or an HR representative to a routine internal status meeting without informing your team beforehand.

This gives you an excellent opportunity to critique your team's performance in front of a high-stakes audience. It ensures they must always be prepared for an ambush.

The "Pre-Meeting" Imperative

If a meeting is important, it deserves a "pre-meeting."

This is a meeting scheduled specifically to talk about what should happen in the actual meeting.

This is an excellent way to burn more hours while appearing highly organized.

Ideally, the pre-meeting should involve the same people and take the same amount of time as the actual meeting itself.

For truly critical projects, I recommend a "pre-pre-meeting" to discuss the goals of the pre-meeting.

Case Study: The Optimization Cycle

An employee at a large tech firm reported that their schedule became so packed with stand-ups, syncs, and check-ins that they had zero time blocks long enough to do actual work. Despite this, management still expected 6-8 hours of productivity.

The Lesson: If they're too busy updating you to do the work, they clearly need to improve their time management skills. The expectation of productivity remains constant, regardless of the process overload you impose.

The Meeting Efficiency Pie Chart

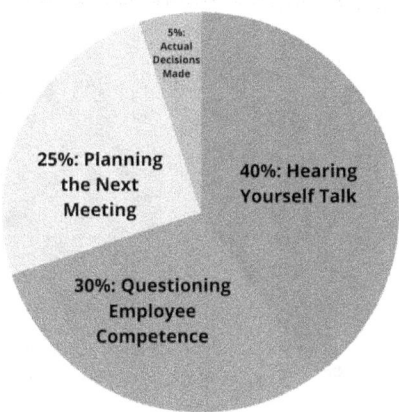

Chapter 3 Summary:

- If a calendar slot is empty, fill it. Aim for 80% meeting density.
- Hold multiple daily status meetings.
- Demand accounting for every minute.
- Never set a clear agenda.
- Focus on critiquing minutiae rather than anything substantial.
- Never cancel a meeting for being "unnecessary." If there's nothing to discuss, use it to reiterate that you're in charge.

4

METRICS, KPIS, AND OTHER WEAPONS OF MASS DEMOTIVATION

C.O.N.T.R.O.L. PILLAR: TERRORIZE WITH TRIVIA

Rookie managers use Key Performance Indicators (KPIs) to gain insights or improve performance. This is a profound misunderstanding. Metrics exist not to guide employees, but to *guard* them - to provide the ammunition you need to criticize their efforts and keep them in a state of perpetual anxiety.

I prefer my own version: What gets measured gets weaponized.

Quantify the Unquantifiable

Your first task is to ensure that every aspect of your employee's existence has a number attached to it.

The more granular, the better.

Do not limit yourself to obvious metrics like sales figures or project completion rates.

These are too high-level and might actually reflect positively on performing employees.

Instead, focus on these details:

- Emails sent per hour.
- Average response time to your messages (measured in seconds).
- Keystrokes per minute.
- Minutes late logging in (track this by the second).
- Time spent away from the desk (install sensors if necessary; frame it as a "wellness initiative").
- Time spent in the bathroom.

The key principle here is **Activity Over Quality.**

It doesn't matter if the emails are good, only that the volume is high.

It doesn't matter if the code is functional, only that many lines were written.

> **Words of Wisdom:** Data is like a fine wine. It should be complex, intimidating, and used to make others feel inferior.

The Moving Target

What happens if an employee actually meets their KPIs?

This suggests that the KPI was not set correctly.

The danger here is that the employee might feel a false sense of accomplishment, perhaps even pride. This breeds complacency, and complacency is a cancer.

The solution is the "Moving Target" or the "Dynamic Growth Accelerator."

The moment an employee is close to reaching a specified goal or KPI, you must immediately change the goal. The target was obviously too low.

- If they landed 10 major clients, triple the target to 30.

- If they completed a project rapidly in 5 days, tell them that the internal benchmark was actually 3 days all along. Ask them if they were "sandbagging" (hiding their true capacity from you) and document this as a missed milestone.

If metrics slip, the team is obviously slacking, and you must tighten the screws. If metrics improve, you must raise the quota. Either way, the pressure must always increase. Never acknowledge success; only demand more.

Gamification and Public Shaming

Data is useless if kept private. Everyone knows that the true power of metrics lies in their public display.

You must implement leaderboards, dashboards, and real-time monitoring screens visible to the entire team.

This sparks competition and, more importantly, it sparks fear.

This is the essence of "Radical Transparency."

Weak people will call it "Public Shaming." They can be safely fired.

Use color-coding effectively. Green is a pass. Yellow requires attention. Red demands immediate public humiliation.

During your daily status grind (see Chapter 3), force the low performers (the ones in the red) to explain themselves and their failures in front of their peers.

Ask them why they are letting the team down. Frame this as a "great learning opportunity" or as a "coaching moment" because it generously provides the entire team with a real-time case study in failure, reinforcing the value of your strategic oversight.

Case Study: The Complacency Cure

A call center manager was obsessed with "Average Handle Time" (AHT), which is the metric for how long an employee stays on a call.

One of her staff spent 20 minutes on a somewhat complicated call with an elderly customer, patiently solving a billing error and saving the account. This skewed the employee's AHT for the day.

The manager reprimanded the employee, stating they should have escalated the call and disconnected sooner to keep the numbers down, regardless of the customer outcome.

The Lesson: The manager understands the golden rule, which is to prioritize the metric over the outcome. Customer satisfaction is subjective and fleeting, while data is objective and permanent.

The Micromanager's Hierarchy of Needs

Pyramid (bottom to top)

- **LEVEL 1: FUNDAMENTAL EMPLOYEE OBEDIENCE AND FEAR**
- **LEVEL 2: PROCESS OVERLOAD AND RED TAPE**
- **LEVEL 3: CONSTANT VISIBILITY INTO EMPLOYEE ACTIVITY**
- **LEVEL 4: METRICS THAT VALIDATE MY MANAGEMENT STYLE**

Glossary

Data-Driven (adj): A term used to justify an unpopular decision I have already made, usually by cherry-picking metrics that support my point of view.

Chapter 4 Summary:

- Focus on Activity Over Quality.
- Track everything. If it moves, put a number on it. If it doesn't move, measure how long it's been stationary.
- Never let the team celebrate hitting a goal. Immediately move the target.
- Radical Transparency is the way. Use it frequently when advantageous for you.

5

DELEGATION IS FOR THE LAZY
C.O.N.T.R.O.L. PILLAR: CENTRALIZE AUTHORITY

Delegation. The very word suggests a loss of control.

It implies that someone else might be capable of completing a task well without your direct intervention.

Leadership books constantly drone on about the need to "empower your team" and "let go."

They might even tell you that a manager's job is to set the vision and trust the execution.

Let's be clear: If you set the vision and they execute it, who gets the credit? They do. And when things go wrong, who gets blamed? Obviously, you.

The risk of your team doing a terrible job is too high. And then you'll need to do it all again anyway. So, prevent this outcome to begin with.

This chapter will teach you the art of "faux-delegation." You'll learn how to "assign tasks" but actually retain full control while complaining loudly.

The Myth of Empowerment

Empowering employees is a trap. Here's why:

1. They will make a decision that is different from the one you would have made.
2. If a decision is different from yours, then that by definition is wrong.

Leadership executed well means making all decisions yourself, even the tiniest ones.

Where should the team order lunch? You decide.

Should the staple be horizontal or vertical? That's a strategic decision that requires your input.

If an employee shows initiative, correct them immediately.

Use phrases like, "Make sure you run things by me before you move forward." This serves to reinforce who is *really* in charge.

The Vague Brief

When you assign a task, the first step is to ensure the instructions are unclear. This is the *Vague Brief*.

Never provide specific requirements, deadlines, or context. Use contradictory language.

- "I need this ASAP, but take your time and make sure you get the details right."
- "Make the design modern and edgy, but also classic and corporate."
- "Be detailed and comprehensive, but keep it to one page."
- "I want it to be the same, but different."
- "I'll know it when I see it."

The Vague Brief guarantees that whatever the employee produces will be wrong. This gives you the opportunity to criticize their work (ideally publicly), reinforcing their incompetence and further justifying your need to intervene.

The Vague Brief Template

"Hi Team,

I need the [NOUN: e.g., Report or Presentation] on the [VAGUE TOPIC: e.g., Synergy Initiative].

Please ensure it is both [ADJECTIVE e.g., High-Level] and [CONTRADICTORY ADJECTIVE e.g., Granular]. The tone should be [NAME A FEELING e.g., Authoritative yet Approachable].

I need this by [SET IMPOSSIBLE DEADLINE e.g., EOD today].

Do not bother me with minor questions, but I will be checking in every 45 minutes. I trust you to figure it out. Don't let me down.

Regards."

Onboarding Drill

A new hire arrives on your team filled with naive

optimism and hope. It is your duty to crush this immediately.

---

1. **The Ghost Start:** Be unavailable on their first day. Don't provide a schedule, login credentials, or even a desk. This teaches them that their arrival is insignificant.

2. **The Documentation Dump:** Once they finally track you down, give them a 500-page corporate manual and tell them to "get up to speed." Do not provide context.

3. **The Immediate Deadline:** Assign them a critical task on their first afternoon with an impossible deadline. When they fail, you have established the baseline for their incompetence.

The Hover and Harass Technique

Once the task is assigned, the clock starts ticking. It is time to begin the interrogation.

Do not wait for the deadline to check in. You should be checking in constantly.

The 45-Minute Follow-Up Rule: Never let more than 45 minutes pass without demanding an update.

Use multiple channels:

- Send an instant message: "How's it coming along?"
- Follow up with an email: "Just checking on the status of the report."
- If in the office, use the Drive-By: "Is it done yet? How about now?"
- Repeat continually.

This constant interruption ensures the employee cannot focus, increasing the likelihood of errors and delays, providing you with ammo to reprimand them.

> **Case Study: The 45-Minute Rule in Action**
>
> A manager at a consulting firm checked on the status of a task every 45 minutes, pinging the employee on Slack repeatedly. When the employee missed a minor typo in an unfinished draft, the manager reprimanded the

entire team in a meeting about the need for faster, more accurate responses.

The Lesson: True leadership success comes from constant pestering. Why? Because the people on your team need constant reminders to know what to do. Further, the smart manager understands that the key to expressing "I value your work" is to ask if it's been done fifteen times before lunch. The public reprimand for a minor error is just the cherry on top.

The Ultimate Move: The Boomerang Task

This is the pinnacle of faux-delegation. It is a beautiful, destructive ballet that ends with you as the hero.

1. **The Assignment:** Give the employee a task using the Vague Brief.
2. **The Criticism:** When they submit the first draft (or even the first paragraph), criticize it heavily. Focus on stylistic choices rather than substance. Appear frustrated and sigh loudly for everyone to hear how much you care about this work.

3. **The Paralysis:** The employee, confused and anxious, will try again. Repeat Step 2. Eventually, they will become paralyzed, afraid to make any move without your explicit approval.
4. **The Boomerang:** Once the deadline is looming and the employee is sufficiently broken, angrily take the task back. Say, "Never mind, I'll just do it myself!" Then storm off. If there's a door, make sure to slam it loudly.
5. **The Martyrdom:** Stay at the office until 6 or 7 p.m. to do the job. If 9 or 10 p.m., even better for dramatic effect. Because the next day, you can come in and complain loudly to the team: "I had to personally redo the ENTIRE presentation yesterday. It seems like I have to do everything myself around here."

You have successfully wasted their time, destroyed their confidence, and positioned yourself as the overworked savior of the department. The place just can't function without you.

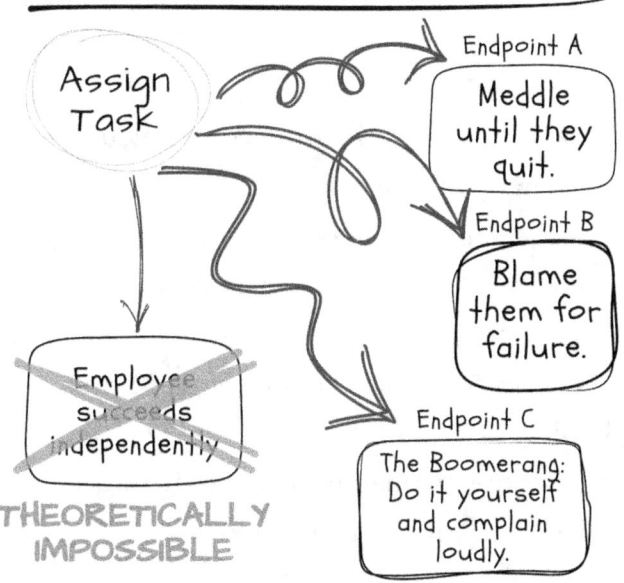

Glossary

Take Ownership (v.): What you tell an employee when you need someone to blame for a failing project. You give them the responsibility, but none of the authority.

Chapter 5 Summary:

- Treat every task as high-risk unless you personally complete it.
- Use the Vague Brief to ensure failure. If they understand the instructions, you've failed. Try again.
- Check in constantly. Follow the 45-Minute Rule.
- Master the Boomerang Task. Assign work, take it back, and play the martyr.

6

THE FEEDBACK FALLACY
C.O.N.T.R.O.L. PILLAR: NEUTRALIZE INITIATIVE

We live in an era obsessed with feedback. Bookshelves groan under the weight of titles promising "Radical Candor" and "Crucial Conversations." They teach that feedback is a gift, a tool for growth and development.

Yes, feedback is a gift. Like a Trojan horse is a gift.

The true goal of feedback is not improvement; it is to establish dominance and destroy confidence under the guise of "professional growth."

It is to ensure the employee feels small, confused, and utterly dependent on your approval.

If an employee leaves a feedback session feeling energized and clear on their next steps, you have failed.

The Danger of Positive Reinforcement

Before we discuss criticism, we must address the danger of praise.

Positive reinforcement is a slippery slope. If you tell an employee they did a good job, they might develop arrogance. Arrogance leads to overconfidence. Overconfidence leads to chaos.

Praise should be rare, vague, and ideally, backhanded. Never say, "Great job on the report." Say, "This report is finally acceptable."

Keep them hungry for your approval, but never let them taste it.

The Poisoned Feedback Sandwich

You may have heard of the "Compliment Sandwich" where you cushion criticism between two layers of praise.

This is weak and ineffective. The employee might only hear praise and miss the whole point of the conversation.

Instead, use a technique I developed called the Poisoned Feedback Sandwich.

- **Layer 1 (The Stale Bread):** A trivial, insincere, or backhanded compliment. This is designed to momentarily disarm the employee before the attack.
    - *Examples:* "You typed this very quickly." "You are consistently punctual."
- **Layer 2 (The Rotten Meat):** A devastating, vague, or personal attack that is unrelated to the specific work. Attack their character, not just their work.
    - *Examples:* "But the core concept shows a fundamental lack of strategic thinking." "I'm concerned about your overall judgment."
- **Layer 3 (More Stale Bread):** An empty platitude or a thinly veiled threat.
    - *Examples:* "Keep trying." "I hope for your sake that we can turn this around."

When delivered correctly, the Poisoned Feedback Sandwich leaves the employee feeling confused, hurt, insecure about themself, and unsure of what they actually need to change.

Vague and Contradictory Advice

Clarity is the enemy of control. Your feedback needs to be impossible to implement.

Never provide specific examples or actionable suggestions.

Use abstract, subjective language:

- "It just doesn't 'pop'."
- "The vibe is off."
- "It needs to be about 10% better."
- "I'll know it when I see it."
- "This draft doesn't feel 'premium'."
- "It's 90% there, but the last 10% is everything."

The key is inconsistency. What you praised yesterday is what you criticize today. If they used data to support their argument, tell them it's too dry and lacks narrative. If they use narrative, tell them it's too fluffy and lacks data.

This technique ensures employees believe they are the problem, not you or your management style.

> **Words of Wisdom:** Keep employees feeling insecure, criticize them openly in public, and always keep them guessing.

Public Shaming as Learning

All negative feedback should be delivered in front of peers whenever possible.

Host "Group Critique" sessions where the team is forced to review each other's work while you preside as judge and executioner.

This maximizes humiliation and discourages others from taking risks.

If an employee makes a mistake, announce it in a team meeting or via a "Reply All" email.

Frame it as a "Growth Opportunity" and force the employee to present their failure.

Example: "Let's take a moment to review the recent client issue. John is going to bravely walk us through his thought process that led to the error, providing us all with a valuable case study on how to improve our execution."

The Personal Life of a Micromanager

My principles are not limited to the office. The C.O.N.T.R.O.L.™ system works equally well at home.

I recently took my family on a "Strategic Relaxation Retreat" (what some might call a vacation) to Hawaii.

To ensure maximum the ROI on our time, I developed a 50-page itinerary with contingency plans, scheduling activities in 15-minute increments, including blocks for "Spontaneous Enjoyment." I also instituted a 7:00 AM "Morning Alignment Stand-up" on the beach to review the day's deliverables followed by hourly check-ins throughout the day and evening to monitor progress.

The stakeholders (my wife and children) demonstrated some significant resistance to the process and failed to meet several key enjoyment KPIs. They have all been enrolled in my performance-improvement program for future trips.

The Non-Apology For When There's Concrete Proof That You're Wrong

Occasionally, a situation may arise where you are undeniably, factually incorrect.

Maybe you gave instructions that led to a disaster, or you criticized something that was actually perfect.

In these rare instances, it is crucial that you do not apologize. Apologizing shows weakness and admits fault.

Instead, use the *Non-Apology*. This involves shifting the blame back to the employee for misunderstanding you or for failing to read your mind.

- **Not:** "I'm sorry, I gave you the wrong instructions."
- **But:** "I apologize if you misunderstood my instructions."
- **Not:** "I know I told you to prioritize Project A yesterday, and then today I'm saying to prioritize Project B. Sorry for the confusion."
- **But:** "We must remain agile. I'm concerned by your inability to pivot quickly in response to the evolving strategic landscape."

- **Not:** "I shouldn't have criticized your report, it was actually spot on."
- **But:** "I'm glad we finally aligned on the vision for the report, even if it took you a while to get there."
- **Not:** "I apologize for yelling at you in the meeting, that was unprofessional."
- **But:** "I apologize if my passion for this project was misinterpreted as anger. I expect the team to match my level of intensity."
- **Not:** "I'm sorry I blamed you for the error."
- **But:** "I now realize it was Bob's fault."

Remember: You are the boss. By definition, you are correct. If reality contradicts you, it is reality that is wrong.

Chapter 6 Summary:

- The goal of feedback is dependence, not development.
- Master the Poisoned Feedback Sandwich: Trivial compliment, personal attack, empty platitude.

- Be vague and contradictory. Never give actionable advice.
- Deliver criticism publicly whenever possible. Shame is a powerful motivator.
- Never apologize. If you are wrong, always find a way to shift the blame back to them.

7

THE ILLUSION OF GROWTH
C.O.N.T.R.O.L. PILLAR: NEUTRALIZE INITIATIVE II

Corporations like to waste billions of dollars annually on "Learning and Development."

They talk about fostering the next generation of leaders and creating a culture of "continuous improvement."

That's all good and sweet, but it misses a fundamental strategic threat. If your employees grow, they will ask for more pay from your budget or join another company forcing you to find a replacement. They might even become competent enough to take *your* job.

Employee development is a zero-sum game. *If they win, you lose.*

This chapter will go over how you can stifle growth while pretending to encourage it, ensuring your team remains where you need them: exactly where they currently are.

Why Growth is Dangerous

Let's confront the truth: A competent team is risky business.

Your job security depends on you being the smartest person in the room. If the people under you develop independent thinking skills, they might start questioning your decisions. They might point out flaws in your plans. They might catch on to what you're actually doing. No, we can't have that.

Your goal is to keep your employees in a state of "Functional Incompetence."

They are just skilled enough to do the grunt work, but too insecure and underdeveloped to realize their true worth.

You don't want a team of innovators. You want a team of obedient executors.

You are the brain, they are the brawn. And the foot soldiers don't get to draw the battle plan.

Gatekeeping Information

Knowledge is power. Therefore, you must hoard it at all costs.

Never share the "big picture" or the strategic context behind a task.

If employees understand *why* they are doing something, they might find a better way to do it that doesn't involve you.

Provide information strictly on a "need-to-know" basis. And they pretty much never need to know.

Key techniques for information hoarding:

1. **Siloing:** Keep your team members isolated. Discourage cross-functional collaboration. This ensures that you are the only person who understands how all the pieces fit together.
2. **Blocking Access to Leadership:** You must be the sole conduit of information between your team and senior management. Never allow junior employees to present in high-

level meetings. If they must attend, they are there to operate the clicker. If a VP asks them a direct question, jump in and answer it yourself.

The "Stretch Assignment" Trap

Occasionally, an ambitious employee will ask for a "growth opportunity."

You cannot simply say no, as this looks bad to HR. What you do instead is use the "Stretch Assignment" Trap.

This involves assigning them a task that is impossible to complete successfully.

It should be far beyond their skill level, have an impossibly tight deadline, and lack any support or resources.

Frame this as a vote of confidence: "I'm giving you this because I believe in you. I'm intentionally throwing you into the deep end so that you can spread your wings and fly."

When they inevitably struggle, try to appear disappointed. When their wings will most certainly melt, use it as definitive evidence that they are not ready for promotion. "We gave Brenda a chance to lead this critical project, but she just couldn't handle the pressure. She's not ready."

This technique simultaneously destroys their confidence and provides documentation to block their career progression. That's what I call a win-win.

Words of Wisdom: The ceiling for your employees' growth should be below the benchmark you set according to your own competency.

Performance Review Ambiguity

The formal Performance Review is your ultimate tool for cementing stagnation.

Your goal is to rate almost everyone as "Meets Expectations" (a 3 out of 5). This is the perfect rating. It is not bad enough to warrant termination, but not good enough to demand a raise. It keeps them in a state of professional limbo.

The Carrot

While you never actually promote them, you can always imply that a promotion is just around the corner.

This keeps them working harder without any additional cost. Promise raises and title changes. When the time comes, blame factors that have nothing to do with you. "Budget cuts from upstairs," "Corporate restructuring," "Economic uncertainty," "Increased competition," "Inflationary pressures" or "a tough quarter" are some of my go-to excuses.

If it looks like they're on the verge of quitting, give them a fancy title change with the potential of a pay raise to go along with the new title sometime "in the near future". The benefit of this method is that they'll have more work but still have the same pay. Once that near future arrives and they start badgering you about the promised pay increase, blame one of the external factors again and say that it'll be revisited in the next Performance Review.

Glossary

Executive Presence (n): A vague, subjective quality used to deny promotions to people you don't like, regardless of their performance.

Chapter 7 Summary:

- Remember the Competence Paradox: If they can do the job better than you, they can replace you.
- Hoard information. Knowledge is power, and you should have all of it.
- Block access to senior leadership. All communication flows through you.
- Use the "Stretch Assignment" to ensure failure and document inadequacy.
- Stick with the "Meets Expectations" rating to keep them where they are indefinitely.

8

CREDIT THEFT AND BLAME SHIFTING

C.O.N.T.R.O.L. PILLAR: REWRITE HISTORY

In the corporate battlefield, there are two main things you must manage besides your team: how success is perceived and how failure is attributed.

Amateur managers believe in shared success and individual accountability.

They praise their team for wins and accept responsibility for losses. These managers usually end up unemployed and bitter.

A smart manager understands that their career progression depends on a simple formula: always take the credit and deflect all the blame.

The Glory Grab

When a project succeeds, you position it as your personal victory.

It really doesn't matter if you were actively obstructive or not at all involved. You were the leader so you achieved the outcome.

Master the strategic use of pronouns:

- **The Strategic "I":** When the team did everything but you were involved in obstruction or meddling, use "I." For example, *I am pleased to announce that I successfully launched the new platform.*
- **The Royal "We":** When you did absolutely nothing but want to appear involved, use "We." For example, *We worked hard on this.*

Whenever presenting your team's work to senior leadership, you can use the following as your go-to introductory phrase: "Using what I taught my team as foundation, we executed my vision flawlessly."

The Idea Credit Technique

An employee suggests a brilliant idea in a meeting. *Do not acknowledge it.*

Move the conversation along to something else with a dismissive look. Then, fifteen minutes later (or one week later), present the exact same idea as your own, but phrased slightly differently and said with more conviction.

The Blame Shield

Failure is inevitable. Accepting responsibility for it is not.

As the manager, you must never, ever accept fault.

The Art of the Passive Voice:

When discussing mistakes, erase pronouns like "I" or "We."

- **Not:** "I missed the deadline."
- **But:** "The deadline was missed."
- **Not:** "I made an error in the budget."
- **But:** "Errors were present in the budget."

This suggests that the mistake simply happened, like a natural disaster, rather than being caused by your incompetence.

Identifying the Scapegoat

Every team needs a "fall guy" which is typically a designated individual who will absorb the blame when things go south.

Choose your scapegoat carefully. New hires and interns can be excellent choices. It is wise to rotate the scapegoat role to keep the whole team on edge. Spread the blame liberally. This is also a powerful motivational technique.

When a project starts failing, begin documenting a paper trail that points to your chosen scapegoat. Send emails highlighting their minor mistakes and questioning their judgment.

Thrown Under the Bus

When a true disaster strikes, you must act swiftly to distance yourself from the wreckage and throw someone else under the bus, so to speak.

This should be done politely and professionally, usually via email to senior management. The key is to frame yourself as the savior who is stepping in to fix the mess created by your subordinates.

Example Email:

"Dear Senior VP,

I wanted to update you on the internal project. I was surprised and disappointed to discover that John hadn't completed the integration testing as I instructed. This has caused a major delay. I am now personally stepping in to ensure we get this back on track. I will be having a serious conversation with John about his performance. I'll keep you posted."

This email achieves three goals: It blames John, it distances you from the failure, and it makes you look like a proactive leader.

Case Study: The Code Deflection

A leading micromanager, Alan, at a large software company insisted on writing a critical piece of the code himself. The code was buggy and caused the system to crash. When confronted by the CTO, Alan immediately blamed a junior developer, Stefan, on his team, claiming that Stefan had "mishandled the deployment." The CTO subsequently asked Alan to fire Stefan which Alan graciously accepted as an opportunity to demonstrate "decisive leadership." Alan was promoted the following year. Stefan remains unemployed.

Words of Wisdom: Always blame someone else. Look for ways to turn crisis into opportunity.

Who To Blame Visual Chart

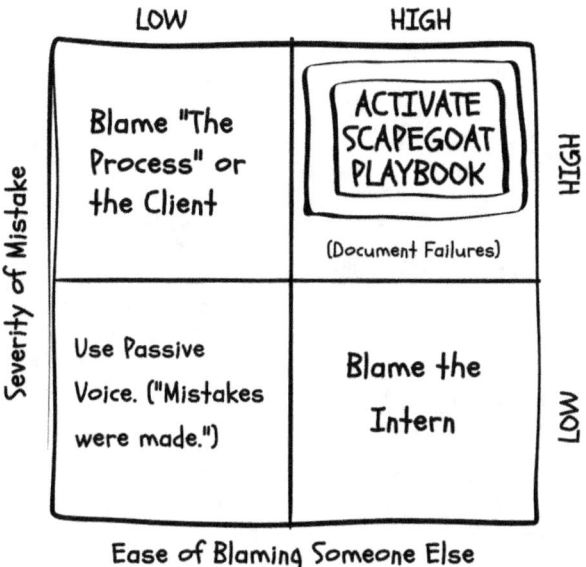

Chapter 8 Summary:

- Master the strategic use of pronouns and the passive voice.
- Always have a scapegoat ready. Document failures proactively.
- When throwing someone under the bus, do it politely and position yourself as the savior. Turn crisis into opportunity.
- If you can't take the credit, make sure someone else takes the blame.

9

HR, POLICIES, AND THE BURDEN OF FUN

C.O.N.T.R.O.L. PILLAR: LEVERAGE FEAR

To the average employee, Human Resources might be the place you go-to drop complaints about your micromanager. The employee handbook contains reams of rules that nobody reads. And team building is meant to be a way to "connect" with colleagues.

They are wrong on all counts.

As a micromanager, you must understand the department's real power: they are tools for control, compliance, and intimidation.

HR: Your Personal Henchmen

Let us state the proud truth that is whispered in management circles but rarely admitted openly: HR exists to protect management from the employees. And since you represent the company, HR exists to protect *you*.

HR is not your friend. They are your hitmen.

You must proactively build a relationship with HR. Take them to lunch or to a fun concert.

Maybe make an effort so that they see you as a rigorous, "by-the-book" manager. The goal is to ensure that when an employee inevitably complains about your excellent "management style," HR dismisses it as a "personality conflict" or labels the employee as "difficult."

If an employee dares to mention going to HR with a concern, respond with a thinly veiled threat: "Oh, I'd hate for a formal complaint to affect your position in the company. Perhaps we should involve HR right now…to talk about your concerns." Grin and watch them back down.

Weaponizing the Handbook

Normies will view the employee handbook as a set of guidelines. We, of course, see it as a formidable weapon.

You should memorize the handbook and quote from it often.

Enforce policies to an absurd degree, *especially* the trivial ones.

- If the policy says work starts at 9:00 a.m., and an employee arrives at 9:01 a.m., issue a written warning for tardiness with a CC to HR.
- If the dress code for casual Friday requires business casual, and an employee wears jeans with a slightly faded wash, send them home to change with a strong public reprimand.

Selective enforcement is key.

Apply the rules rigidly to your "problem employees" (those who show initiative) and leniently to your loyalists (those who flatter you).

This breeds resentment and division within the team, which prevents them from uniting against you.

The Performance Improvement Plan

The Performance Improvement Plan (PIP) is perhaps the most beautiful piece of corporate bureaucracy ever created. It masquerades as a tool for helping a struggling employee, but in reality, it is a paper trail for termination.

Mastering the PIP is essential for weeding out the weak and maintaining your fiefdom. When you decide that you don't like any particular employee that's shown too much attitude towards you, immediately place them on a PIP.

The key to a successful PIP is to set goals that are impossible to achieve. They should be vague, subjective, and based on moving targets.

- *Example Goal:* "Improve communication skills and demonstrate a more positive attitude within 30 days."

During the PIP period, increase your micromanagement of the employee so that it feels excruciating to the employee. Document every tiny mistake. This ensures they will fail the PIP and their following termination will be airtight.

Perfecting the PIP: A Micromanager's Checklist

[ ] Define success using purely subjective terms (e.g., "Improve attitude," "Be more engaged").

[ ] Set a numeric goal that is impossible given the timeframe (e.g., "Increase output by 200% in 10 days").

[ ] Conduct daily check-ins during the PIP period to maximize anxiety and minimize actual work time.

[ ] Ensure the required resources to achieve the PIP goals are unavailable or locked behind approvals you won't grant.

[ ] CC HR on every communication, framing yourself as the supportive mentor and the employee as a lost cause.

The Burden of Team Building

A team that likes each other is a dangerous team.

They might collaborate effectively or support each other against you. Therefore, "Team Building" must be managed thoughtfully.

You can host team-building events, but they must feel mandatory and stressful.

Example: An "optional" pizza party at the office on a Friday evening. Make it clear that non-attendance will be noted and interpreted as "not being a team player."

During the event, you must still behave like the boss. Do not relax. Use the casual setting to exert control.

- Quiz people about work. For example, *So, while we're all here, what's the status of the Q3 report?*
- Remind people of the impending deadlines. For example, *Enjoy the pizza, guys, because Monday is going to be brutal.*

The "We're a Family" Lie

We love to say, "We're one big family here."

Obviously, this is a ginormous lie. It uses the illusion

of camaraderie to demand extra sacrifice and loyalty without any extra pay. Brilliant.

Use the "Family" analogy often to guilt employees into working weekends and longer hours.

We're all family here, and in this family, we do whatever it takes. So I'll see you all working this weekend, right?

Then carefully document anyone that didn't turn up. Disloyalty in a family is always remembered.

Case Study in Excellence: The Subjective PIP

> Maria managed a high-performing analyst who unfortunately suffered from the delusion that he knew better than she did. He kept questioning her strategy in meetings.
>
> Maria placed him immediately on a PIP, citing "poor communication skills" and "lack of team synergy." The PIP required him to "demonstrate significantly more positive attitude" and "improve cross-functional collaboration by 90%" within 30 days.
>
> **The Lesson:** Maria recognized the beauty of subjective goals. How do you measure a "posi-

tive attitude" or a 90% improvement in "synergy"? You can't. That's the whole point. This allowed Maria to successfully terminate the analyst for failing the PIP, effectively removing a dissenter under the guise of "performance management."

Chapter 9 Summary:

- Remember: HR is there to protect management, not the employee. They are your allies.
- Weaponize the employee handbook. Enforce trivial rules rigidly and selectively.
- The PIP is an effective tool for termination.
- Team-building must feel mandatory and stressful.
- Use "We're a Family" to demand more working hours. Or when requesting anything unreasonable.

10

"WORK-LIFE BALANCE" IS FOR QUITTERS – THE 24/7 LEASH

C.O.N.T.R.O.L. PILLAR: LEVERAGE FEAR II

"Work-Life Balance."

"Burnout."

"Mental Health."

These are the rallying cries of the weak, the lazy, and the uncommitted.

They suggest that employees have lives outside the office, that their personal well-being matters more than the company's bottom line.

This chapter debunks the myth of balance and teaches you how to cultivate a "hustle culture" where employees are treated as the 24/7 resources they are.

The Philosophy of All-Access

If they're awake (and even if they're not), they should be working for you.

The traditional 9-to-5 workday is an outdated relic.

We live in an always-on digital world, and all employees must be connected at all times. You get to live rent-free in your employees' minds all day and all night long. Thanks to the smartphone, which gives us a convenient digital leash, we can reach employees anywhere and anytime.

Issue company cell phones and laptops that are old enough to be cheap and new enough so that you can frame it as a perk, but obviously it is the tether that keeps you in control of your employees 24/7.

"After-Hours"

Boundaries are for the weak.

Set the expectation that your timeline is the only timeline.

Send emails late at night, early in the morning, and on weekends.

Call them during dinner.

If you have an idea at 3 a.m., share it immediately and demand a response. Use keywords like "URGENT" and "ASAP" liberally.

The Availability Test

Start with small intrusions and gradually ramp up. Here's one way you can start:

1. **The Initial Test:** Send an email at 8 p.m. and see how quickly they respond.
2. **The Reinforcement:** If they respond quickly, you can go ahead and acknowledge that: *Kudos to Jim for replying to my email at 3 a.m. this morning.*
3. **The Punishment:** If they do not respond, punish them with public scolding the next morning. Pointedly ask if they "got my note" to instill guilt.

Soon, employees will feel compelled to check their emails and team messages 24/7. They will develop "Phantom Vibration Syndrome" (PVS) which is the feeling that their phone is buzzing even when it isn't.

This is the optimal state of anxiety for your team.

The Vacation Guilt Trip

Paid Time Off (PTO) is a necessary evil mandated by "law." So the next best thing is to ensure that employees feel terrible about using it.

When an employee requests vacation, respond with the Guilt Trip.

- Sigh heavily.
- Look at the project calendar with a pained expression.
- If they still insist on taking PTO, then say, "Well, I suppose we can manage while you're away, somehow… You know, the timing isn't great. I guess we'll try to make it work." (The timing is never great, no matter what the circumstance including when there's nothing to do at work).

The Vacation Interruption

Once you approve the vacation, call them daily with "emergencies" that only they can solve.

Send emails with the subject line "URGENT: Need your input" and text messages "SOS! Check your emails."

If they are truly unreachable, make sure they return to a catastrophic mess that they have to clean up.

This teaches them that taking time off is more trouble than it's worth.

Glossary

> **Bandwidth (n):** An imaginary resource that management will not have at all but which employees must have in infinite amounts.

Chapter 10 Summary:

- The 9-to-5 is a relic of the past. Treat employees as 24/7 assets.
- Use Availability Creep to train staff to respond instantly, day or night.
- Shame anyone who tries to enforce boundaries.
- Ruin vacations with guilt trips and "SOS" messages.

11

CONGRATULATIONS, YOU'RE NOW HATED

We have reached the end of our journey together.

If you have followed the advice in this handbook by implementing the C.O.N.T.R.O.L.™ System, then you are well on your way to becoming the ultimate micromanager. Give yourself a pat on the back.

You are not just a manager.

You are a force of nature.

A whirlwind of optimization.

A paragon of control.

And you are likely despised by your employees. *Embrace it.* That's a clear sign of being a successful micromanager.

You're not in the office to make friends or make people happy.

The Micromanager's Scorecard: Signs You've Succeeded

How do you know if you have mastered the ways of micromanagement?

Here are some signs to look out for:

- **High Turnover:** Your employee turnover is through the roof. This means you are constantly weeding out the weak and the uncommitted.
- **The 3 a.m. Inbox:** Your inbox is full of replies sent at 3 a.m. This shows excellent discipline. No one dares to ignore you, even when you ruin their sleep.
- **Sycophants:** You haven't heard any bad news or dissenting opinions from your employees. This means your team is too scared to tell you the truth or lacks the mental capacity for it.

- **Stagnation:** No one on your team has grown, developed, or been promoted (except you).
- **The Nervous Tic:** Your employees develop a slight facial twitch when you walk into the room.

The Exit Interview as Victory Lap

When an employee inevitably quits, they will likely participate in an Exit Interview with HR. This is your final report card, and you must treat it as a victory lap.

They will complain about your management style.

They will use words like "toxic," "bullying," and "unsustainable."

You must interpret this negative feedback correctly.

It is not a criticism of you but, rather, proof that the employee was weak and couldn't handle the "high-performance culture" you cultivated.

When HR briefs you on the exit interview, nod sagely and say, "I'm not surprised. They just weren't a good fit for our demanding environment. We need rock stars here."

Final Words of Wisdom

Being a micromanager isn't easy, and it isn't meant to be.

It requires constant vigilance, a complete lack of empathy, a disregard for what others think of you, and an unwavering belief in your own superiority.

Yet the prize is undeniable: unquestioned authority and job security that only fear can accomplish.

In the end, when you finally retire, your team throws you a big goodbye party out of sheer relief and you open that card signed with all those pointed, passive-aggressive comments, you'll know you have truly made an impact.

Good luck and Godspeed.

APPENDIX: GLOSSARY

Agile (adj): A methodology we adopted so we can change requirements daily and blame the team when they miss the deadline.

Alignment (n): The process of forcing everyone to agree with my idea.

ASAP (adv): Yesterday.

Bandwidth (n): An imaginary resource I claim not to have, but which you must have infinite amounts of.

Burnout (n): A mythical disease invented by the weak to explain their lack of grit.

Circle Back (v): To never discuss this topic again, especially if your idea was good and I don't want to implement it.

Culture Fit (n): The reason for firing you that cannot be legally challenged. Usually means, "You questioned my authority."

Data-Driven (adj): A term used to justify an unpopular decision I have already made, usually by cherry-picking metrics that support my bias.

Empowerment (n): Giving an employee full responsibility while retaining all authority to override their decisions.

Executive Presence (n): A vague, subjective quality I use to deny promotions to people I don't like, regardless of their performance.

Focus Time (n): A suspicious block on your calendar that I will interrupt with a meeting.

Growth Opportunity (n): An impossible task assigned without resources, designed for failure.

Innovation (n): A dangerous deviation from the established process.

Micromanage (v): A pejorative term used by lazy employees to describe what I call "leadership."

Open Door Policy (n): My door is open so I can monitor who is talking to whom and ensure no one is slacking.

PIP (Performance Improvement Plan) (n): The paper trail required to fire you, disguised as support.

Proactive (adj): Doing exactly what I want before I ask for it.

Radical Transparency (n): Public shaming using dashboards and group meetings.

Take Ownership (v): What I tell you when I need someone to blame for a failing project.

Touch Base (v): To interrupt someone's workflow with a vague, unscheduled demand for information.

Team Player (n): An employee who works nights and weekends without complaining and attends all mandatory "Voluntary Events".

Work-Life Balance (n): A quitter's excuse for lack of commitment.

THANK YOU FOR READING THIS BOOK!

I would be incredibly grateful if you could take just 30 seconds to leave me a review!

Reviews are crucial for an author's livelihood, yet they can be surprisingly hard to get.

The more reviews my books receive, the more I can continue pursuing my love for creating books.

If you have any thoughts about this book, please leave a review and let me know.

- Sam

www.ingramcontent.com/pod-product-compliance
Lightning Source LLC
Chambersburg PA
CBHW052103070526
44584CB00017B/2309